Choose Your First Product

4 Easy Steps to Find and Validate a Humble Product Idea

Leon Bambrick

LEON BAMBRICK

Copyright © 2018 Leon Bambrick

All rights reserved.

ISBN-13: 978-1987475357
ISBN-10: 1987475356

CHOOSE YOUR FIRST PRODUCT

for Sharon

LEON BAMBRICK

CONTENTS

DEDICATION 3
ACKNOWLEDGMENTS 7
INTRODUCTION 9
CHAPTER 1: GETTING STARTED 11
    YOU AND YOUR PRECONCEIVED NOTIONS 13
CHAPTER 2: THE GOAL 15
    SHOULD YOU USE AN NDA TO PROTECT YOUR IDEA? 18
CHAPTER 3: INTRODUCING THE TOAD SYSTEM 21
    OVERVIEW OF THE TOAD 24
CHAPTER 4: TOAD STEP 1: FIND YOUR TARGET MARKET 27
    WHAT IS A MARKET? 29
    IDENTIFY YOUR TARGET MARKETS 32
    MARKET FINDER WORKSHEET 34
        Market Finder: Hobbies and Interests 37
        Market Finder: Family and Friends 38
        Market Finder: Work and School Experience 39
        Cross Out Groups You Dislike 41
        Cross Out Groups That Are Not Groups 42
        Why Start With Markets? 48
        A Word About TAM, SAM, and SOM 49
    FIND YOUR PEOPLE 52
    MARKET EXPLORER WORKSHEET 54
        Market Column 56
        Website Column 56
    HAVE YOU FOUND YOUR TARGET MARKET? 62
CHAPTER 5: TOAD STEP 2: FIND COMMON OBSTACLES 63
    TECHNIQUE 1: FROM PERSONAL EXPERIENCE 66
        MeWare: Software For One 68
        ProbLog: A Log of Your Problems 69

No Pressure No Diamonds 70
TECHNIQUE 2: BY QUALITATIVE RESEARCH 72
   "Coding" (AKA "Tagging") 74
   The Perils of Tagging 76
   Take Note of Jargon 79
TECHNIQUE 3: POST QUESTIONS AND QUESTIONNAIRES 80
   Who Should You Ask? 82
   Asking People Directly 83
   Asking Via Surveys 84
HAVE YOU FOUND A PROBLEM WORTH SOLVING? 86

CHAPTER 6: TOAD STEP 3: PROVIDE AN ANSWER 87

WHAT SORT OF SOLUTION ARE YOU AFTER? 89
CONSIDER EXISTING SOLUTIONS 91
CONSIDER ACADEMIC RESEARCH 92
ATTEMPTING THE IMPOSSIBLE 95
HAVE YOU SOLVED YOUR PROBLEM? 96

CHAPTER 7: TOAD STEP 4: TEST FOR DEMAND 97

WHAT IS A DEMAND SIGNAL? 99
   Just One Tweak! 101
THREE EXCELLENT WAYS TO TEST FOR DEMAND 102
TECHNIQUE 1: POST INFORMATION TO A HIGHLY RELEVANT FORUM 103
TECHNIQUE 2: LANDING PAGE WITH PAY-PER-CLICK CAMPAIGN 106
TECHNIQUE 3: CONDUCT A CROWDFUNDING CAMPAIGN 109
   Why a Kickstarter Campaign is a Good Idea 110
   Why a Kickstarter Campaign is a Bad Idea 111
HAVE YOU MET YOUR GOAL? 113

CHAPTER 8: NEXT STEPS 115

APPENDIX A: TOAD OVERVIEW 117

APPENDIX B: REFERENCES 119

APPENDIX C: IMAGE CREDITS 123

ABOUT THE AUTHOR 125

ACKNOWLEDGMENTS

No book is an entirely solo expedition, and I'm grateful for help from a very nice group of people.

Sharon Hennessey gave me the benefit of her insight and her patience.

Simon Harriyott delivered many thoughtful improvements.

Douglas Finke asked all the right questions at precisely the right time.

Patrick Johannessen and Joseph Cooney chimed in with quite a few valid points.

Richard Mason rushed in at the last minute and lent a hand.

Looking back, I can't be certain that I really did any of it. I'm very proud of what Sharon, Simon, Douglas, Patrick, Joseph, and—eventually—Richard have achieved and hope you enjoy it too.

LEON BAMBRICK

INTRODUCTION

Let's start with the context:

You're on the planet known as Earth, orbiting a gentle sun. It is the 21st century. And you want to create a product.

It will be a "digital" product of some sort: it may be a website or an app, it may be a book or a course. You will market it and deliver it over the internet.

You've dreamed of embarking on this marvelous journey for far too long. Finally, you are ready to get started.

But first, you need to find the mythical and elusive "idea." You've looked for ideas and found only stinkers: too big, too old, too weird, too hard, too risky.

What you need is a straightforward process that makes it easy to find a good idea.

Ah, look at this! You're reading a book! Not just any book either. This book. A book that will give you:

---

*Four Easy Steps
to Find and Validate
a Humble Product Idea*

Are *you* ready? I'm ready. Let's go.

LEON BAMBRICK

CHAPTER 1: GETTING STARTED

Here's where the big mistakes are made. Not later on, not a year from now. But right here. At the very start. Before you've even chosen an idea. I want you to pause at this moment. This is the dangerous part, the part worth doing properly.

Have you noticed that modern software draws you into its embrace via the gentlest movements? Whether we're playing games, following tutorials, or getting cozy with accounting software, the first moments begin with a lovingly-crafted "onboarding" process that coaxes you forward, one tiny step at a time. First, they present a very simple challenge. You get that right and they immediately give you a gold star to reinforce how clever you are. You stumble over the next little jump and they congratulate you more. Slowly your skills and experience grow as you progress through a steady series of dopamine hits until you're hooked. How easy, how fun!

Bad news, my friend. Creating a product is *nothing* like that.

It doesn't start off easy and rewarding. It starts with the nastiest challenge of all. That's where you are right now. Faced with a task that is very close to impossible.

The diabolical thing about your situation, when choosing a product idea, is that if you race into a decision now it could be years before you realize just how terrible your idea was.

The later parts of the product journey involve "micro-optimizations." You'll find local minima, tiny improvements, quick wins; but the initial choice of what product you build is a truly **global** optimization. Do this wrong and you're wasting your time and money. You'll throw away weeks, months or decades of your life. All that will be left of your mighty dream will be a "Domain for Sale" web page, or, if you're lucky, an interview at *Failory*.

You and Your Preconceived Notions

There is one other possibility I need to address before we get started. Many of you will already have a specific "idea" that you are hoping to productize. And you may be quite attached to that idea.

I won't attempt to tear your precious pre-existing idea out of your fingers. But you should find the process used in this book will also be sufficient to help you assess your current idea. This book will present you with questions and help you answer them. By applying those questions to your current idea, you may find ways to tweak your idea (perhaps reducing the scale of your grandiose ambitions) or to twist your ambitions (perhaps targeting it toward a more cohesive market). It's possible you may decide to put your idea on hold for now, and work on a simpler idea. You may even keep your original idea intact, but with a crystal-clear idea of how to bring it to fruition.

CHAPTER 2: THE GOAL

Before you embark on the quest to find the perfect product idea, I want you to pick a *pragmatic* goal. I can't jump out of the book and force you to do this, but I want you to consider picking the following goal. It's the goal that Rob Walling chose when he set out on a journey that resulted in his successful product *Drip*. Rob's goal?

> *I wanted to find 10 people who would be willing to pay a specific amount for the product once it was complete.*
>
> —Rob Walling[1]

It's so simple and so practical. 10 customers, at a specific price. Why 10 people? Why not 3? Or 300?

10 is an excellent number because it's so modest, so humble and yet big enough to be real. Even though it's a small number, it's much bigger than the number of real customers that most people enlist before they launch themselves (and their life savings) into a hare-brained

scheme.

Most people think about how much money they will spend, or wildly postulate about potential customer numbers, but cannot for the life of them produce a short list of real, committed customers. Instead their plan is:

> *"Jump off the cliff and learn how to make wings on the way down."*
> *—Ray Bradbury*[2]

Jumping off a cliff and making wings on the way down is a *terrible* approach. Starting with a goal such as "Find 10 real customers, before you commit to an idea" is a better approach.

Rob's inspiration was Jason Cohen of *A Smart Bear* who gives this compelling argument for finding 10 real customers *before* you build:

> *If you can't find 10 people who say they'll buy it, your company is bullshit.*
> *—Jason Cohen*[3]

It's easy to get hooked on an idea, inside your own head, or inside the echo-chamber of your own inner cabal.

Finding 10 *real* customers who *demand* the product, is a way to ground the idea in reality, right now, rather than three years down the track after you've exhausted yourself. It's also a fantastic starting point to help you develop the confidence and the ability to talk to real customers.

If you can't find 10 people, that's the best news of all.

Why? Because at that point you've done precisely *nothing* towards building it. Look at all that time and energy you've saved. Well done you!

The other advantage to finding customers as early as possible is that it requires overcoming the most common fear of all:

> "But won't people steal my idea!?"
> —Everyone who ever came up with an idea.

We love our ideas and feel they are the most precious things in the world. We fear that as soon as we share an idea with other people they'll pick it up, run away with it, and beat us to the market.

Let me reassure you now: the sort of people who are capable of reaching the market with a well implemented idea are NOT sitting around without ideas, just waiting to hear your untested and unproven idea. They are already overloaded with ideas, and if they did decide to suddenly turn to the dark side and imitate an idea, they would pick any one of the million ideas that are already demonstrating a **profit**.

Should You Use an NDA to Protect Your Idea?

One of the ways people respond to this fear of idea-stealing is by insisting that people sign a Non-Disclosure-Agreement (NDA) before they hear the particulars of the idea. There are two groups that use NDAs: gigantic companies use them and complete amateurs use them.

Gigantic companies operate on a different level to you and I, their reasons don't apply to us. But beginning entrepreneurs use NDAs to allay their fears, not because of any realistic risk.

Here's a quick way to test if NDAs are valuable. Fire up your trusty browser and go looking for "horror stories" about times when someone regretted not having an NDA. You won't find any stories like that (barring a few written and embellished by law firms selling NDAs). Contrast this with some other protective device, such as "backups." If you go looking for "horror stories" by people who regret not making a backup, you will find them everywhere, written by normal people. Not just being pedaled by vendors of backup-related products. Backups address a real problem, NDAs only address a fear.

If we agree we're looking for an idea, which you won't be afraid to share and you've set a practical goal, such as "10 paying customers," then how are you going to get there?

Luck? Prayer? Brainstorming? No. To get to this goal, I've built a process, a system. Come along with me now. I want you to follow the TOAD.

CHAPTER 3: INTRODUCING THE TOAD SYSTEM

It took a long time to come up with a fitting acronym that rolled off the tongue like "TOAD." The TOAD, the wonderful, mystical TOAD. I'm sorry that it happens to be a kind of gross and unloved animal, but that's why I've chosen a cute TOAD image to represent it. And there's a nifty slogan as well:

If you want to meet
your Prince Charming
you'll have to kiss
a lot of **TOADs**

What does TOAD stand for?

- **T**arget market
- **O**bstacle
- **A**nswer
- **D**emand

Those are the four things you're going to find, in their most efficient order. The next four chapters cover these in detail.

Target Market: As this is your *first* product, we'll make the marketing easy by sticking close to home. To achieve this, we'll interview **you**, to find the markets that suit you best. I'll help you to explore these markets, get a feel for how each of them works, and pick one or two to focus on. If things go wrong in a later step, you'll return to this step, so I'll give you worksheets for making notes you can use again and again.

Obstacles: Next, I'll help you look for problems that people often experience in the market you've chosen. I'll teach you a range of techniques to get at these problems. Once you've found a juicy enough problem you've completed this step. But again, you'll be ready to repeat this step as needed. It's worth taking the time to get the right product idea, so we're not going to rush.

Answers: Now that you've found a problem, well known to your target market, you're going to solve it. Sounds hard, doesn't it? If you're a software developer you're already an expert at solving specific problems. But even if you're not: the problem (or problems) you found above are in a market that you understand, so you have a home-ground advantage. If the problem turns out to be beyond your abilities, I have a few ideas that might help, and you always have the possibility of going back to the first two steps to find a *different* problem. I'll ask you to do the least work possible to prove that you can solve the problem because you're not ready to commit to this idea, not yet. There's one more crucial step before you're certain this is going to be your product.

Demand: Armed with knowledge that you can solve a real

problem experienced by your target market, you now conduct some *tests* to see if there is genuine *demand* for your solution. This is the bit that everyone misunderstands, and either refuses to do at all, or does at the wrong time. We're looking for a "Take My Damn Money!" response from the target market related to *your* specific solution to their problem. Once you've got that, you can commit to your product idea and proceed with great confidence.

You may have to go through parts of this cycle several times before you find your product. It will be a wise investment of your time.

Overview of the TOAD

Here's a handy diagram to give an overview of the TOAD system

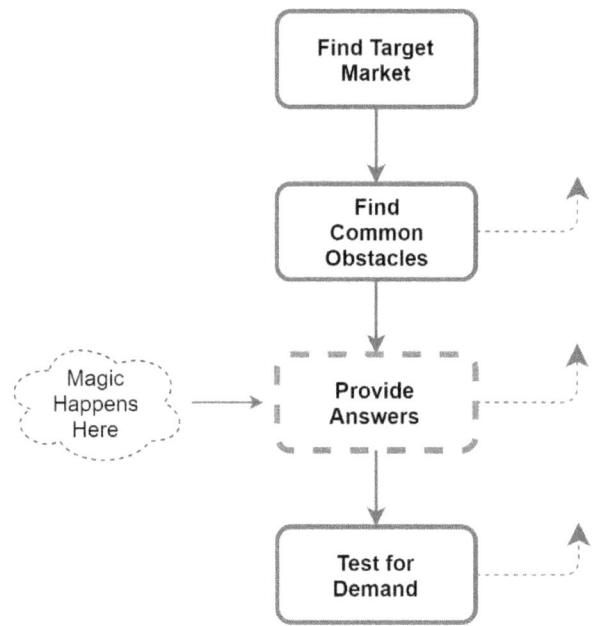

There is a more detailed diagram at the end of this book, which includes all the sub-steps.

For each step I'll give you three different techniques. Pick the one way that works best for you. If you get stuck on any one technique, I've got at least two others you can try.

Why provide many techniques for each of the four steps? Because you **must** find all four before you can commit to a product idea. These alternative paths exist as a guarantee that you can find a way to continue without getting blocked.

Enough preamble, let's hop to it.

CHOOSE YOUR FIRST PRODUCT

CHAPTER 4: TOAD STEP 1: FIND YOUR TARGET MARKET

Target • Obstacle • Answer • Demand

You Are Here

Target, eh? What sort of a target? An archery target? Are we going to be firing arrows? No, no we are not. It is a different sort of target, and I'm going to have to say a particularly filthy word:

Marketing.

The target we're looking for is a Target Market. As an engineer I have an occupational aversion to the word "marketing." And yet I've learned enough about it that I no longer fear it in the slightest.

What is Marketing primarily about? Is it about inserting popup ads on web pages? Is it about putting commercials on during the Super Bowl? What is this marketing thing all about, and how can it help you in a practical way?

Get ready for some mind-blowing information: marketing is primarily about... *markets*.

Those things you think of when you hear "Marketing" are really *Marketing Communication* ("MarCom") or, more simply, *Promotion*.

But "Marketing" and "Promotion" resemble an iceberg.

Promotion is the most visible part of marketing, the part of the iceberg that protrudes above the surface. But the largest part of marketing, the part below the surface, is about trying to truly, deeply *understand* the market. That's the sort of marketing you need to do *before* you build a product.

What is a Market?

Picture a small medieval farmers' market. People travel to it from the surrounding countryside to buy or sell their produce. Is that a market? Yes and no, what we've described are three things: a place, people, and produce. Which one is the market? The "place" is not the market, it's a "marketplace." The "produce" is not the market; the word we use for those are "products." What about the people, what are they? The word we use to refer to the people at a marketplace is "market." The **people** are the market!

Our working definition of a market is: a set of people who identify as a group and share a common interest. When we say "What does the market think?" or "How will the market respond?" We mean, what do people think? How will people respond? And, specifically, people with our common interest.

Now bear with me for a moment. While we're picturing this medieval farmers' market, let's make a few observations.

What sort of behavior is exhibited by these local peasants? Do they silently move up to a stallholder, select their

CHOOSE YOUR FIRST PRODUCT

produce and quietly move away? No, they do not. They are never quiet. Marketplaces are noisy, busy, crowded, and boisterous. Do they look at each other? You bet they do! They noisily discuss their purchases, haggle over prices, and ask many questions as they inspect the merchant wares. They boast about their best purchases, and they give and receive bushels of information. This medieval farmers' market is full of data. Big noisy data.

Cut forward to the modern era and much has changed. The products we're interested in are digital, and the marketplace is online. It might be Amazon, eBay, an app-store, or a website. The people are not physically in the same place. But what happens to all that chatter? Does it disappear? Is it a relic of the past? Absolutely not.

The chatter is louder than ever. It is the Amazon product reviews, the eBay reputation, the Facebook threads, the tweets, the forums (oh God, the forums) the rumbles of Reddit, the app-store stars and reviews, the blog posts, the YouTube unboxing videos, tutorials and walkthroughs, and of course the comments on YouTube. And when Amazon, eBay, Facebook and so on are gone, the market chatter will continue elsewhere. Market chatter is eternal and always exists somewhere. Knowing where to find that chatter is a big part of the journey. We'll come back to this at each step of the product development lifecycle.

First, we have to find your people, your potential markets. And after that I'll help you observe the market chatter so you can zero-in on the best target for your first product.

Identify Your Target Markets

There are three distinct places where you can look for your target markets. You may not look in all three, but I'll ask you to consider them all rather than getting blocked and abandoning the search altogether.

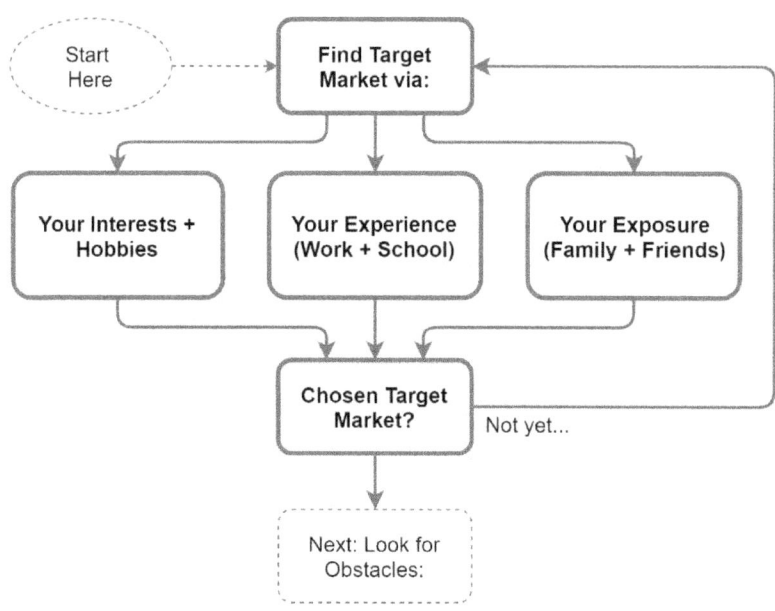

CHOOSE YOUR FIRST PRODUCT

Take the "Market Finder" exercise sheet, available as a PDF here:

<u>YourFirstProduct.com/Tools/MarketFinder</u>

...and printed inline on the next page.

Market Finder Worksheet

Hobbies+Interests	Family+Friends	Work+School Experience

CHOOSE YOUR FIRST PRODUCT

The Market Finder worksheet is a simple table with three columns. I want you to fill it out in as much detail as possible. You're connected to more markets than you realize.

The three columns are:

1. Hobbies and Interests
2. Family and Friends
3. Work and School Experience

These columns represent the three different approaches for finding target markets.

You can reproduce the Market Finder on a piece of paper in under five seconds.

In each column I want you to list every industry, group, or profession you've ever interacted with.

Before I go any further, I need to explain something about this exercise.

Imagine the following scenario. You've heard good things about a particular restaurant so you make a booking and go there. You order their famous signature dish and it arrives at your table. It looks and smells amazing. You post a photo to Instagram with this caption:

"Looks delicious! #foodie"

...and then you go home without eating the meal.

If you read this book without attempting the exercises, you are exactly like that starving Instagram foodie. The purpose of a meal is to be eaten. The lessons you can learn from this book are only available if you attempt the exercises.

For this exercise you need to list every group of people where you have a personal insight. Why not start instead with the most lucrative groups in the world? Or the biggest groups? Why worry about *personal insight*? A professional marketer can target a group of strangers. But we are not professional marketers. As amateurs we need every advantage we can find. Focusing on groups we're connected to will make every decision easier. And in the course of developing a product there are thousands of micro-decisions.

When filling out this sheet, you need to turn off your inner critic. Don't think ahead. Don't censor yourself or apply any filters that reduce the number of industries you write down. There will be time for filters later. Right now, you need to be expansive. Let the ideas flow and let one memory lead to the next. Tangential markets are allowed. You will need to think hard to recall all the roles and industries you've worked with.

Market Finder: Hobbies and Interests

Under "Hobbies and Interests," enter every last hobby you've ever enjoyed.

You know Kung Fu? Then write down "Kung Fu." You sing and dance? Then write down "singing" and write down "dancing."

You don't need to be *good* at these things but you need to be *genuinely* interested in them.

Are you a cat person? Write "cats." Are you a dog person? Write "dogs." A keen worm farmer? Write "worms."

"Hobbies and Interests" don't have to be your *current* hobbies. Think back to interests you've enjoyed in the past, perhaps when your life was less busy. They *all* count.

Market Finder: Family and Friends

Under "Family and Friends," write the industry or professions of any family and friends you are in regular contact with.

If your family business is the making of shoes, then write down "Shoe makers." If someone close to you is a doctor, then write down "Doctor." If all your friends are violinists, write "Violinists."

Market Finder: Work and School Experience

Under "Work and School Experience" write every industry or profession you've experienced first-hand through work (or, for younger players, through school).

What industries have you worked in? If you are a software developer, you should also write down "software development," and any particular flavor of programming, or any particular roles in the software industry that you've worked with. Like accounting or law, software development gives you broad exposure to other "vertical" industries. Write down all other industries you've experienced.

(A "vertical" industry is any specialized industry. If you write a booking system for dentists you are targeting a "vertical," but if you write a word-processor for *everyone*, you are targeting a "horizontal" market, i.e. everybody.)

As you think of items for one column, it may unlock memories or reveal items to write in other columns. If you can't unlock enough memories, try writing on a blank sheet of paper: first write down the year you were born and each year since then. For some of us, this step alone can take a while. Then write a word or two about what you know or recall from each year, sketch out the briefest outline of your autobiography. This will give you a broad survey of your life and help unleash more potential markets to engage with.

Once you've reviewed your life to date and considered all your associates in the world, you'll have a sheet something like this:

Market Finder

Hobbies+Interests	Family+Friends	Work+School Experience
Guitar/Bass	Physiotherapy	Oil+Gas
Parenting	Real estate	Retail
Blogging	Electrician	Gambling
Novel writing	Musicians	Resource Planning
Product bootstrapping	Tutoring	Data Integration
eBook Writing	Teaching	C# Dev
Karate		Data Quality Management
Vinyl LPs		SQL Server dev
Mathematics		Web dev
Board games		GIS/Geo-spatial
Dad jokes		Software lifecycle
Photography		Kanban
Robots		Version control
Lego		Consulting
Fractals/Recursion		Work from home
Genealogy		Remote work

It should contain quite a few potential markets. Perhaps you already feel there is one market that really stands out from the rest. Even still I believe the next few points are relevant. We are going to remove some terrible markets from your list of candidates.

Cross Out Groups You Dislike

When your product is a success, you will deal with many support requests from these people, so make sure these are people you feel happy to work with.

Take a group from the list, for example "Real Estate Agents." Imagine you walk into a social gathering, and it's filled with Real Estate Agents. How does this make you feel? Do you think:

> *"Ahhh, these are my people, I am so happy to have wandered into this room!"*

...or do you turn and run? If you would turn and run, then cross them off the list. Those are **not** your people and you should **not** build a business for them.

As obvious as this seems, it's exactly the kind of mistake people make every day. Apply this test to every group on the list. If there are no groups left, then go back to the start of the chapter and try again.

Cross Out Groups That Are Not Groups

When choosing your market, you want a group of people who "behave like a group." They are "cohesive" and display group dynamics.

You're ultimately looking to find a group of people you can sell your product to. At a practical level this will let you "target" them with advertisements.

What is this "group behavior," "group dynamics," and "cohesiveness?" I will give you some positive examples and one negative example.

Positive examples: Fans of the band *Grateful Dead* refer to themselves as "deadheads" and they continue to do this long after the band themselves stopped performing. Fans of the group *Insane Clown Posse* call themselves "Juggalos" and have their own festivals, and a wide array of face and neck tattoos to show their affiliation. Those are very strong examples of group behavior and cohesiveness.

Here's a negative example. The group "Business Analysts" might sound like a fantastic target customer. A naive and *serious* businessman would be forgiven for assuming that "business analysts" are a better target market than "Juggalos." But let's see what the research reveals, *inside of 20 seconds*.

Run a search for "business analyst software" and this is what you see:

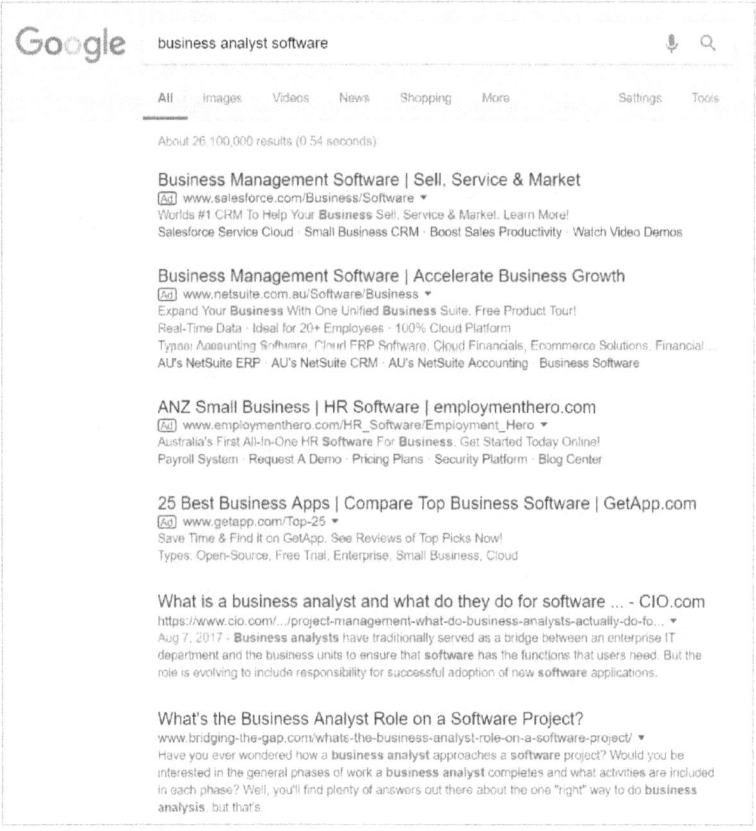

The first warning sign is in the Google Ads themselves.

There are four of them, and they are not targeted at "Business Analysts" at all, instead they focus on "Business Software."

The organic results, below the ads, also fail to address the exact search clause. Instead, they are answering a more general question, "What *is* a business analyst?"

The inherent existential angst of that question ("What *is* a business analyst?") is a clear sign that there is no "Group Cohesion" here. Worryingly, there are four advertisements in a row, showing that there is strong competition over this search term, despite the poor cohesion of the marketplace. This would make advertising expensive, despite the poor targeting. And similarly, the organic search results themselves are not focused on the search query itself. Given that no one has written a well-ranked article about software for business analysts, it's clear that no content author is chasing this traffic.

Long ago, in the first years of the new millennium, a search result like the one shown above would've been an ambiguous signal. It might have meant that there was a hole in the market: no one had yet gotten around to writing products and content targeted at "Business Analysts." But in recent years, it is implausible to find that the millions of content farms have overlooked a search term used by a large and lucrative set of people. Hence, from this result alone, I can guess right away that very few Business Analysts are getting neck tattoos that say "BA for Life." And I would cross them off my list as a group to target. So long, BAs.

CHOOSE YOUR FIRST PRODUCT

Contrast this with the results achieved when we search for "Dentist Software," shown below. The ads are about software for dentists and the organic results are about software for dentists. These are more promising signs if you're looking for a group worth marketing to. It also indicates that "dental software" is a somewhat crowded market and I'll address that in a moment.

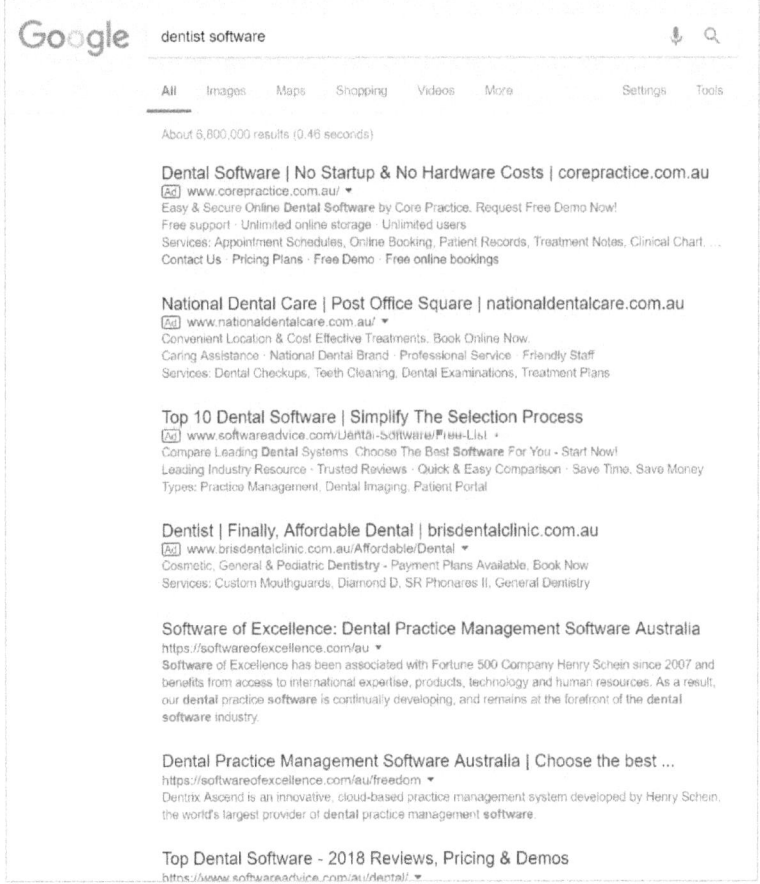

Don't be scared off by a seemingly crowded market.

45

Wherever there is demand there is likely to be existing supply of some sort. Paul Graham neatly summarizes the meaning of a crowded market in this quote from his essay "Startup Ideas."

> *"A crowded market is actually a good sign because it means both that there's demand and that none of the existing solutions are good enough."*
>
> *—Paul Graham*[1]

And this quote from Marc Andreessen also explains the surprising connection between supply and demand:

> *"In a great market—a market with lots of real potential customers—the market pulls product out of the startup.*
>
> *"The market needs to be fulfilled and the market will be fulfilled, by the first viable product that comes along."*
>
> *—Marc Andreessen*[2]

Or as Slava Akhmechet expressed the same notion:

> *"The innovation market is efficient... if there are no startups in a given market, it's overwhelmingly probable that market conditions are not hospitable."*
>
> *—Slava Akhmechet*[3]

CHOOSE YOUR FIRST PRODUCT

The upshot of which is that the existence of products is itself a good indication that a market exists. This is an important concept to understand and, in my mind, quite unintuitive.

This doesn't mean that your exact product idea will have direct competitors. It only means that products will exist that cater to the same market—the same people—to whom you wish to appeal. Those other products could just as well be your *partners* as your competitors.

Using the above process, you can whittle down your list, until it contains only those groups that **behave** like groups.

Why Start With Markets?

This question of group behavior strikes at the heart of what we're looking for, and helps us answer the question "Why start with markets anyway?" Why should a product developer begin by choosing a market? Can't that come later?

It might seem like a better idea to create a product that appeals to ***everybody***. But if you invent a product that applies to everybody, it is very hard to ***sell***. Instead of advertising to a small, focused group, you are in the arena of "broadcast" marketing: buying television ads, advertising at the Super bowl, taking out a full-page ad in the New York Times. Since the product applies to everyone, there is no single group that should be passionate about it. Your potential customers are unlikely to talk to each other about the product, as it's not tied to anything about themselves; it will need to be very "remarkable" for them to remark on it at all.

A cohesive group is the opposite of this situation. They are cheap to reach via targeted advertising as they "hang out" in predictable places. And they love discussing everything about the thing which binds them together.

A Word About TAM, SAM, and SOM

TAM, SAM, and SOM are concepts that people often use when assessing potential markets. We will mostly ignore those concepts, but they're Kind of a Big Deal, simply because beginners can waste time worrying about them. I'll give a brief explanation of TAM-SAM-SOM. Here we go.

What is the TAM? Well, let's say that you've decided to write software for dentists. The TAM is the "Total Available Market," or: how many dentists are there in the world? You do some internet research and find there are an estimated 10 million dentists in the world. Great, you rub your hands together with glee. (All figures have been fictionalized for illustrative purposes and should not be used as a basis for any serious business decisions.)

Whenever people start sizing up industries, I'm reminded of Lloyd in *Dumb and Dumber* explaining the amazing business opportunity he's discovered to his passenger Mary:

"And best of all, worm farming is a seventy-five-thousand-dollar-a-year industry. I wouldn't mind having a piece of that pie, if you know what I mean."
—*Lloyd from Dumb and Dumber*[4]

But wait: TAM-SAM-SOM, what's the SAM? The "Serviceable Available Market." You're planning to advertise over the internet, and only 20% of the dentists out there use the internet, then your SAM is 2 million. Still not bad, but what's the SOM?

The SOM is the "Serviceable Obtainable Market." You're going to advertise on Dentists-Dont-Bite.com, and it only has 3 actual dentists (and 10 thousand fake dental hygienist bots... don't ask) so your SOM is exactly 3.

The TAM-SAM-SOM is most relevant if you are planning to

invest tens of millions of dollars in the hope of growing your product into a *globally dominant* market saturator with a multi-billion-dollar valuation.

For a Humble First Product, you only need to consider the last term: SOM, Serviceable Obtainable Market. Who can you truly reach?

Find Your People

Armed with your list of target markets (having removed a few duds) it's time to identify the places where they ask questions online and gather some information about these places.

Information gathered now will help you throughout the rest of your product journey. It will help you find and understand "Obstacles" in the next section. It will give you somewhere to connect with potential customers and build your reputation in the community. It will give you a place to verify the market's opinions on your decisions. It will help you finesse the language to use on your marketing materials before you launch (and after). It may also be a place where you can buy targeted ads later.

But most importantly, it will enhance your understanding of these markets and. And if you still have more than one or two markets remaining, it will reveal which markets are worth your time.

Your investigations will uncover a lot of information. I have a piece of paper to help you structure your notes. You're free to create your own variation of this page.

The three-column **"Market Explorer"** is available here:

CHOOSE YOUR FIRST PRODUCT

YourFirstProduct.com/Tools/MarketExplorer

You may wish to print your own copy. A copy is also provided on the next page.

Market Explorer Worksheet

Market	Website	Notes

CHOOSE YOUR FIRST PRODUCT

There's nothing special about this three-column sheet. Instead of firing up the old printer you might as well draw up your own copy on a blank sheet of paper. It's not DRM protected and you do not need a degree in "PDFology" to interpret it. There is something wonderful about three-column sheets. You can do anything with a three-column sheet of paper: you can plan a wedding or prepare to save the earth from its eventual demise in the fiery expansion of the sun. In this case, we'll learn about markets.

The three columns are:

- Market
- Website
- Notes

Enter a target market in the first column. In the second column enter some related websites and forums for that market. In the third column enter any notes or facts you can uncover about those websites. In particular, record notes about the liveliness and reach of the website.

There will be an explosion of data from left to right. The first column will only have a few markets listed. The second column will have many websites per market. The third column will have many facts per website. There's no particular structure to the notes you enter in the third column. Record any pertinent facts you discover, particularly about the scale and "energy" of the website.

Here is an example I filled out earlier:

Market Explorer

Market	Website	Notes
C# Programmers	reddit.com/r/csharp	Subscribers: 56,000 Online now: ~193 Posts per day: ~12 Rules: reddit.com/r/csharp/about/rules
	reddit.com/r/dotnet	Subscribers: 29,000 Online now: ~95 Posts per day: ~8 Rules: reddit.com/r/dotnet/about/rules

Market Column

The market column is just data you carried over from the previous exercise. It could be Dentists, it could be Lion Tamers. It's a group of people.

Website Column

Finding the best sites for reaching your target market online can be tricky because the internet is, frankly, a cesspool. Take C# Developers for example. If you search for "C# Forums" you won't find the popular destinations for C# developers, what you will instead find is "Who is the best at SEO for this particular search term?"

Despite this, there is a simple trick to knowing where C# developers go. The trick is to *be* a C# developer. The same trick applies to every other niche market you have on your list. Because these are all markets that you are personally connected to, you shouldn't need to rely on Google to find where they hang out. You've already been to many of the right places, due to your existing knowledge and experience in this market. If you have *no idea* where they hang out online, then you may not know enough about this market and it probably doesn't belong on your list in the first place.

Perhaps you are not a member of the group but know a lot of people who are. For example, you're the only non-doctor in a family of doctors. That's OK. In that case, you need to grab a family member, throw them to the ground and sit on their chest until they answer your every question, starting with: where do you go online to talk about this doctoring business?

In addition to online meeting places, it's excellent to also find "real world" meeting places. Are there user groups, clubs, conferences, gatherings of any sort where your people come together? You can find such groups via *Facebook*, or through *Meetup.com*. Take a few minutes to locate such groups and take some notes about where and when they meet, how large or small they are, and whether people say they're worth attending. You don't need to attend the groups in person (not yet) but should get an overview of the liveliness and scope of these groups.

For finding online groups, the two largest collections of groups online are *Facebook* and *Reddit*. I'll briefly discuss conducting market research at each of them.

Exploring Facebook

Facebook makes it very easy to find groups via a search. When you perform a regular search, you can restrict it to groups with one click. For example, here is the URL for a search for "Photography."

facebook.com/search/groups/?q=**photography**

The search results give you an immediate overview of:

- How many members are in the group?
- How many posts are made per day on average?
- How many people near you are in the group?
- Which of your Facebook friends are in the group?

Those are the exact sort of top-level facts you want to write down about these groups.

Clicking through to a group gives you a more accurate view of these top-level statistics.

For example, I found a Worm Farming group with about 100 posts per day. I suspect that worm farming may be a more lucrative market than Lloyd from *Dumb and Dumber* would lead us to believe.

Clicking through is dangerous though, because at this point we're looking for top-level information. We don't want to be drawn too deep into any one group.

Exploring Reddit

If you haven't done so already, it's worth looking at "The Front Page of the Internet," *Reddit*[5], to see if there are any "subreddits" (groups inside Reddit) that pertain to your target market. I know, I know. Reddit can be terrible, but I'm not asking you to move to Planet Reddit, just to include it in the places where you conduct your market research. Many of the smaller subreddits are charming little places. And the number of people at reddit is fantastic.

For example, using the *Subreddit Search Tool*[6] to hunt for "C#" quickly revealed the "CSharp" subreddit[7] a group with over 40,000 subscribers.

A search for ".net" showed a group with only 700 subscribers. Searching for "dotnet" brought me to a group with 20,000 subscribers[8]. So, I can ignore the first group and only record facts about the second group.

(If you're a programmer it's worth knowing about the general group "/r/programming"[9] which has 750,000+ subscribers)

If you start with one subreddit you can find other related subreddits by using *RedSim*[10], a tool custom built for this purpose. Given any subreddit, it analyzes the subscriber base to find other subreddits they commonly follow.

Once you've found a few groups of interest you can then create "multireddits" to view them together. Like this:

CHOOSE YOUR FIRST PRODUCT

reddit.com/r/**csharp+dotnet**

… i.e. by concatenating the names of the groups, separated with a plus sign, after "reddit.com/r/"

Reddit makes it very easy to see the number of subscribers, and the number of people currently online for any subreddit. That top-level information is helpful for making quick comparisons and decisions.

You can use other tools for analyzing subreddits. For example, visiting *Reddit Metrics*[11] you can gather more specific info about how the subreddit has grown over time. And to find the best time of day to post you can use *Later for Reddit*[12], for example:

dashboard.laterforreddit.com/analysis/?**subreddit=csharp**

Have You Found Your Target Market?

After all this sleuthing you should've found your most promising target market and know exactly where that particular creature likes to hang around online.

If you haven't discovered a good market yet, go back and give it another go. I've given you three easy ways to find markets and a few ways to rule out markets, so you really have no excuse if you still haven't found a good market. Your problem now might be an abundance of markets, in which case you'll need a better way of ranking them. All else being equal, pick the one you understand best. It will give you a home-ground advantage like nothing else.

Having chosen a market, everything from here forwards will be easier. The hardest thing when building a business is all the decision making. And every decision will be simpler when you can turn the question into, "What would suit my target market best?"

The next step of the TOAD journey will be performed completely hand-in-hand with your future customers. Let's jump in.

CHAPTER 5: TOAD STEP 2: FIND COMMON OBSTACLES

| Target • Obstacle • Answer • Demand |

You Are Here

Once you've identified a good market, it's time to look for common "obstacles" in that market. What problems do your target market face?

What do I mean by obstacles? I mean problems or barriers or limitations that stop a member of that target market from becoming the successful person they want to be.

If the target market is, for example, "photographers" then what are the obstacles that must be overcome to be a *better* photographer? What are the time-wasters that stop them from excelling as a photographer? What are the lessons they have to learn before they can advance their skills to the next level? What are the problems they encounter, or the questions they stumble over, again and again, as they try to succeed with their ambitions?

To help find these obstacles, I've described three quite different techniques you can use. This way if you dislike one technique you can try the next. There's no getting stumped or blocked with the TOAD system.

Find Obstacles

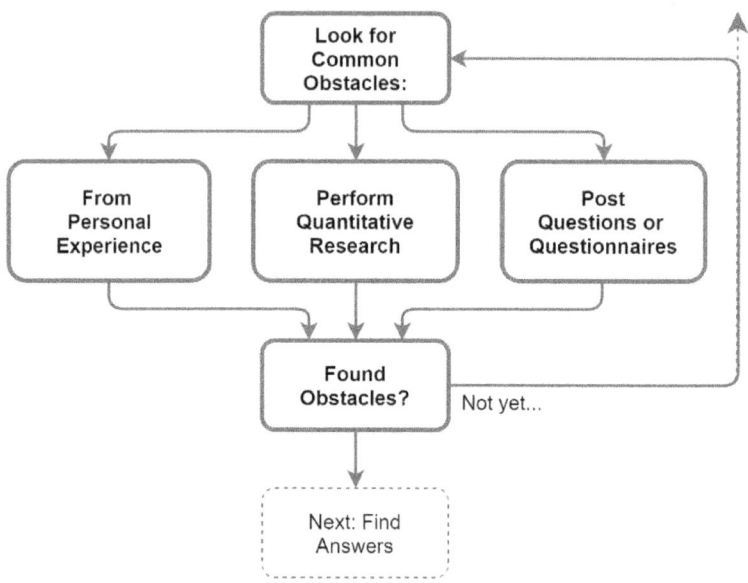

The three ways to look for Obstacles are:

1. From personal experience
2. By qualitative research
3. By asking people (through questions or questionnaires)

You can perform all three, you can combine them together, or you can do just one of them. Whatever it takes to find a problem worth solving.

The first two techniques are "passive"—you don't need to

interrupt anyone, you don't need to interact with humans, you don't need to "put yourself out there." The third technique is "active"—you need to socialize with people. If you're an introvert you might gravitate toward the first two techniques. But I encourage you to move beyond passive approaches and embrace active techniques as well. You will soon learn much.

Before you are free from this little book, in the "Demand" part of the TOAD, you will need to use *active* techniques (there is no alternative). Now let's dig into these three ways of finding real problems.

Technique 1: From Personal Experience

Assuming you're targeting a familiar market, the simplest approach is to look at problems you've experienced yourself.

This technique is often called "scratch your own itch" which really downplays the importance of the technique. Many great businesses began with people solving their own problems. Personally, all my own products to date have arisen from scratching my own itches.

If it's a problem you've suffered from personally, then you know it is a real problem, not an imaginary one.

> *"Why is it so important to work on a problem you have? Among other things, it ensures the problem really exists. It sounds obvious to say you should only work on problems that exist. And yet by far the most common mistake startups make is to solve problems no one has."*
> *—Paul Graham*[1]

Working on your own problem you'll have a home ground advantage in understanding the problem. You'll probably have a rich understanding of the problem's nuances and side-effects.

There are two specific dangers that are worth mentioning

when you focus on solving your own problem:

1. You may be solving a problem that is *only* experienced by yourself. Your TAM, SAM and SOM are all equal to just one customer: yourself.
2. You may solve a common problem in such a way that it is only appealing to yourself.

In the words of David S. Platt, "You Are Not Your Customer"[2]. You have less in common with the final paying customer than you think: for example, *they* are not willing or able to stop, solve the problem, and turn it into a product. Your unique perspective can make your own needs quite different to all your future customers.

For both of these reasons there are more steps to undertake before you can safely commit to building a product. The Demand step in Chapter 7 in particular is designed to uncover assumptions, limitations, and misguided notions that arise from your myopic vision.

MeWare: Software For One

I have many small inventions which I use constantly, but which I don't sell as products, as they are only suited to my own use. "**MeWare**" like this is worth building and maintaining, for your own benefit, and I highly recommend it. But just because you use a tool, even frequently, doesn't mean it is worth productizing.

As alluded to above, a test for demand will show which MeWare products are worth productizing, and which can remain as MeWare.

ProbLog: A Log of Your Problems

Once we've tolerated a problem for long enough, we become blind to it; we become complacent about the problems we face every day. One way to make familiar problems visible again is by keeping a detailed log of your work, with a particular emphasis on any *obstacle* which arises and prevents you from achieving your intermediate goal. If you work hard and are very observant you might find as many as 20 obstacles in a single day. You'll certainly find at least 5 obstacles per day. You don't need to keep recording this log forever. You might just keep it for two weeks, or for the first few hours of the day, each day for a month.

You can also use an "experience sampling method" to uncover the problems you face in great detail. To use this technique, you set an alarm to go off at random times throughout the day. Each time the alarm goes off you immediately fill in a short form, explaining what you're doing, what problem you're overcoming, what you're procrastinating about (if anything), and a few other questions. Random sampling alleviates the need to perform continuous monitoring. If you extend the experiment for longer you will get more insight into recurring patterns. (This technique is particularly helpful for uncovering bad habits, and their causes.)

No Pressure No Diamonds

There is another way to unearth your own problems (and to rapidly invent solutions to them), and I hesitate to suggest it because it is not a sustainable long-term practice. But since I've used it successfully, and never seen it explicitly talked about anywhere else, I ought to share it. It is alluded to in the sayings "Necessity is the mother of invention" and "No Pressure No Diamonds."

Three of the products I've released came from ideas that first presented themselves to me during difficult situations: times when I was very overcommitted and expected to achieve about three times as much in a single day as was humanly possible.

One Friday I was racing to meet a deadline, a deadline I knew I could never fulfill, and I was also expected to produce a detailed timesheet of my week. I was being pulled in two directions at once. It had been such a hectic week that I'd taken no notes at all, and I had no time to try and work out where my time had gone. What was normally just a nuisance (filling out my timesheet) was suddenly a *crisis*. And this crisis put the inventive part of my mind into overdrive. I immediately invented the idea that would become *TimeSnapper*[3].

There are identical stories of impossible deadlines behind the creation of the first prototype of *NimbleText*[4] and *NextAction*[5]. When you try to do more than is possible, you quickly discard all irrelevant work, discard all the busy work, the paper shuffling and the accidental complexity. What's left is the essential problem, and within that essential problem it becomes clear which part of the work is the critical path. Some tiny ancient part of the brain springs into action, and suddenly finds a way to solve the essential problem, in the same way that a desperate trapped rat suddenly finds a hidden store of energy or an unexpected escape route.

Notice that the new ideas do not necessarily benefit you at the time. You suddenly think of the perfect tool that would help you climb out of the current hole you are in. But you don't have the time to actually build the tool there and then. All you can do is sketch a few quick notes about the tool you need, and hope to come back to it later when things are quieter.

To harness this technique you need to impose deadlines on your normal work, the harsher the better, and then you'll gain a clear picture of which part of the work really creates a bottleneck. As mentioned, this is not sustainable, so I wouldn't recommend living in that situation for an extended period of time.

Technique 2: By Qualitative Research

Qualitative research is exploratory research, where you don't know what you're going to find in advance of finding it. It is a way of reviewing and sifting through a large amount of raw material with a view to uncovering useful aspects of the material in a time-efficient manner.

I encourage you to perform qualitative research in the web forums and marketplaces you discovered during the "Target market" part of the TOAD. The type of qualitative research described here is similar to that used in social sciences, though it also has some features in common with work that falls under the blanket term of "Market Research." It is a difficult thing to explain, though easy to demonstrate. It is at once both objective and subjective.

Your goal, while performing this qualitative research, is to find recurring problems experienced by your market. What are the problems that are encountered again and again? Not only do you want to find common problems, but you want to find ones that evoke a strong response from the market: for example, strong emotional words. You may have to dig quite far back in time before you begin to see patterns, or you may watch the forum for a considerable time, looking at new posts as they arrive.

Qualitative Research is touched on briefly in the literature on Lean Validation. But for a much more comprehensive system, look at the work of Amy Hoy. She's created a method of qualitative research called "Sales Safari"[6]. With her business partner Alex Hillman, they've worked with hundreds of clients to turn it into a very robust method which they teach as part of their popular course "*30x500*"[7].

"Coding" (AKA "Tagging")

Qualitative researchers are often faced with mountains of data to analyze, much like the situation you will find yourself in.

To deal with this situation, they've refined a process known as "coding" but which has very little in common with the sort of "coding" familiar to software developers.

When qualitative researchers talk about coding it is more like "tagging" or "annotating," in which you are identifying particular traits within a document or interview.

In the description that follows, I'm going to use the term "tagging" for what a qualitative researcher would call "coding." The process is as follows:

You move through the document, tagging any word, phrase, or sentence that expresses the particular feature you're looking for. If you're tagging for "sentiment" then you would find any words or phrases that indicate a sentiment and tag them accordingly. The tag might be "Angry" or "Happy," or some other concise term.

You can picture a researcher reading through the text from an interview or a group discussion, with several different colored highlighters in their hand. If they see a happy phrase, they mark it with their yellow highlighter, if they see an angry phrase, they mark it with a pink highlighter. When they are done, they scan back over the document and make notes about what was highlighted. They might just record how many tags of each color were made. Or they might extract all the highlighted words, their locations, and see what new research questions this creates in their mind.

If you're tagging for many different features, you might create more complex tags. For example, if you're tagging for political orientation as well as emotions, you might have tags such as "Political: Conservative" and "Emotion: Worry." If using highlighters, you'd quickly run out of colors. Hence, it's good to organize your research digitally.

There is a wide variety of software available for full-time qualitative researchers[8]. Much of this software is highly complex and boasts all sorts of specialist features to help sift through audio files, video files, web pages, PDFs and every other format imaginable. For an amateur researcher, like you or I, general-purpose software is perfectly adequate. *Evernote*[9] and *OneNote*[10] are two well-known note taking applications that are very suitable. Or a plain text editor (like *Notepad++*[11]) will suffice. Qualitative notes are quite unstructured and it's good to give yourself a lot of freedom. (I've tried writing special software to help with tagging and storing research notes, but the challenge proved too great in the time I allocated to it.)

The Perils of Tagging

This business of tagging comes with its own specific set of occupational hazards. There are two hazards that I will alert you to, as you're likely to encounter both. I'll use *Flappy Bird*[12] to illustrate; you should navigate between these hazards by putting in enough effort, *but not too much*.

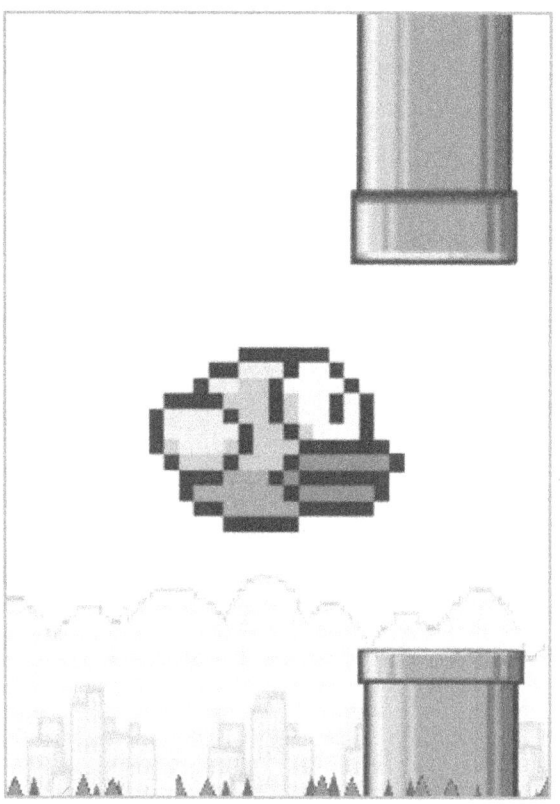

Don't Be Too Passive

If you are too passive when surveying the information, you will end up reading and consuming and never extracting the benefits or finding the emotions and problems.

That is the plight of the "wantrepeneurs," spending too much time letting the information wash over them, without ever absorbing it or acting on it. You're not here to read, you're here to collect evidence to support your product ambitions. Don't lose site of the goal.

Don't Get Hooked In

The opposite problem is when you are "hooked in" by the material you are trying to study.

Instead of looking for surface features, like emotions, problems, and jargon, you instead engage with the material and try to solve the problems that are listed, you become absorbed in the minute details, you follow all the links that are mentioned and lose sight of your research topic.

This is much harder to overcome, and to some extent, it is a good thing.

I assume you're not a serious ethnographic researcher performing a rigorous academic study into the secret life of forum dwellers. You're always allowed to interact with the forums and websites you are studying. I would definitely recommend that you join these forums, provide simple answers where you can, and, in particular, aim to be a beneficial contributor to the community. Which also raises a related point: sometimes it is necessary to join a forum (or Facebook group) before you can see all the content.

But don't spend so long doing these things that you fail to pursue your initial research goals.

And, one last point: don't *ever* get into an argument with people on forums. No matter how *wrong* they are, or what sort of irrational responses you receive, do *not* argue on an internet forum. Please. (I say this with the unique zeal of a reformed sinner).

Take Note of Jargon

Another side-effect of tagging something like a forum is that you can gain a strong understanding of the *jargon*, the terminology used by the target market. Take careful note of this jargon, as this is the best language to use for your website and other marketing materials you produce along your product journey.

The three features you need to identify are "problem," "emotion" and "jargon." Each time you find an example of the above you want to record where you found it, and a snippet large enough to provide context.

As you start to find different examples of the same problem, you group those together. Where you find a strong emotion tied to a problem, you take special note of that and record it under the problem you have found.

Later you should be able to review your notes to find not only which problems are the most common, but which problems inspire the most passion.

These are good problems to solve.

Technique 3: Post Questions and Questionnaires

The above two methods are passive, but it's perfectly OK to take an *active* approach to searching for problems worth solving. That's right: you can straight up *ask* people.

Some commentators are skeptical about this "asking people" idea.

> *"If I had asked people what they wanted, they would have said a faster horse."*
>
> *—Attributed to, but not actually, Henry Ford*[13]

They caution you that people lie, people don't know what they want, people try to give answers that please you, and so forth. Asking people just doesn't seem very *scientific*: it's too likely to confound the study. But asking people is amazing! Just putting a question into words, ready to ask a human person, can really straighten up your curly thoughts.

My answer to the "don't listen to your customers" dilemma is this:

> *Listen to your customer's problems, don't listen to your customer's solutions.*

For asking "online" there are two basic approaches. You can write to a forum with questions that create discussion right there inside the forum. Or you can create a survey and ask people to fill out the survey.

Both approaches are valid. Each is covered in more detail below.

Who Should You Ask?

You can ask people you know or you can ask strangers. You can ask people inside your target market or you can ask people outside your target market. People outside of your target market are not useful at this stage. And people you know are more likely to say things they think you want to hear. So, the best people to ask are relative strangers inside your target market.

There are a lot of places that are sympathetic to the questions of up-and-coming entrepreneurs. For example, at *Hacker News*[14] there is a section for asking questions:

news.ycombinator.com/ask

But I caution you against asking questions at general places. It's better to direct your questions toward members of your target market.

In particular, you should ask at all the locations you found during the "Market Explorer" exercise.

Reddit allows "self" posts where you can ask a question of a given subreddit. If you are asking a well-chosen group (not a general "startup" or "marketing" group) then this would be a perfect place to ask. Similarly, any Facebook group you are targeting would be open to the kind of question or survey you are asking here.

Asking People Directly

The basic open-ended question is:

> *As a xxx what is a problem you face all the time?*

The exact manner in which you phrase the question will be specific to the audience you are addressing.

Or if you've already got a specific problem in mind, ask:

> *It seems like yyyy is a problem for xxx's. How do you deal with yyyy?*

...phrased in an audience-appropriate way.

People love to talk about themselves, and they love to complain, so you should get an informative response. When people begin to respond, you can draw them out, asking for more detail about their experiences.

If it's a real problem, they'll be dealing with it in a lot of different ways and you'll get a wide variety of answers. Everyone will have their own solution. You'll also see strong emotions about the problem. If you don't see any of these behaviors, then the problem is not a powerful one for the audience you've reached.

Asking Via Surveys

There are so many tools for creating surveys online that I can't even begin to offer you a survey of the field (pun intended). I will only give you my conclusions.

In the early stages of your business I recommend using *Google Forms*[15] to perform surveys. It's free, easy to use, and doesn't limit the number of answers you can collect. Google Forms store their data in a spreadsheet at *Google Sheets*[16]. From there you are free to do anything you want with the data. It's also possible to write scripts that make things happen when new survey results are posted, although that's a bit advanced for the stage we're discussing now.

Professional survey tools, such as *Survey Monkey*[17] and *TypeForm*[18] include a free-tier, though there are serious limitations for this free tier. For example, they might allow only 100 responses per month. It's in the paid tiers where these tools begin to shine. For a low monthly fee, they allow you to create customized forms, with complex workflows, and integrated email marketing features. Once you're an established brand I recommend switching from Google Forms to TypeForm as your survey provider. TypeForm have achieved something remarkable with their surveys. If you haven't seen it, be prepared for amazement.

But back to Google Forms. If you've never created a Google Form before, take a few minutes to create one now. It's quite straightforward and perfect for marketing surveys.

You can embed your survey into emails, onto webpages, or share it in a forum (or other social media) just by posting a URL. They're very versatile.

Remember to ask people for their email address as part of the survey. This way you can follow up for more information, and possibly develop a friendly relationship with the most insightful people.

Have You Found a Problem Worth Solving?

After using one or more of the techniques above, you should have found at least one problem that is worth solving. If you've found more than one, then it's fine to carry them all forward until such a time as a clear winner emerges. Having extra problems to think over is a good use of your spare time.

If you haven't yet found a problem worth solving, keep looking. If one technique doesn't work for you, try the next. If none of the techniques work for you, supplement them with your own techniques from independent reading. In such a case, please write and let me know what techniques you've come up with. Some people collect stamps, I collect techniques.

Finally, if you've exhausted your interest in a market without finding any suitable problems, you can go back to your Market Finder exercise to pick a different market and continue the process from there with a new target market in mind. It's unlikely that there are no good problems left in the world.

CHAPTER 6: TOAD STEP 3: PROVIDE AN ANSWER

Target • Obstacle • Answer • Demand

You Are Here

Now that you've identified a problem or two, it's time to go ahead and solve it.

Depending on the problem you're attempting to solve, this can get very tricky.

Here's an "overview" diagram, as provided for each step of the TOAD. But unlike the other overview diagrams, this one does not provide very much insight at all.

Find Answers

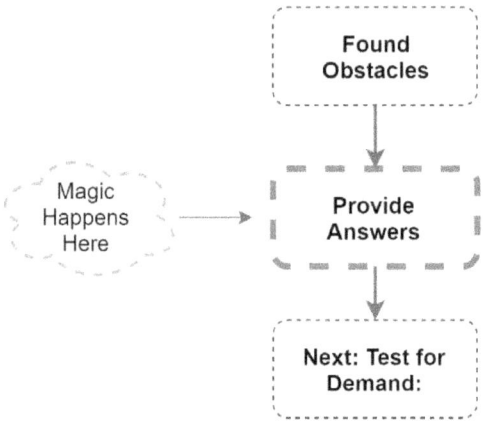

That "Provide Answers" box does look a *little* tricky.

If you're the same caliber of genius as the physicist Richard Feynman, you can simply apply the Feynman algorithm:

> *The Feynman Algorithm:*
> 1. *Write down the problem.*
> 2. *Think real hard.*
> 3. *Write down the solution.*
>
> *—According to Murray Gell-Mann*[1]

If you're not quite at that level of genius then you may be happy to hear about some more practical ways of solving problems. But first, I want to give you a clear picture of what it means to "solve" a problem.

What Sort of Solution Are You After?

Solving the problem doesn't mean building a polished end-product that encapsulates the solution to the problem. Solving the problem doesn't mean coming up with all of the marketing materials and a snazzy name and a killer radio advertisement. Solving the problem doesn't mean nailing every edge case and every detail.

It doesn't mean you need to develop a "minimum viable product" (MVP). The solution you are working toward falls very far short of being viable as a product. It's barely even a prototype: more like a prototype of a prototype. We're talking *ROUGH*.

The only thing that this solution must provide is **proof**. It must prove to yourself that, given extra polish and effort, it would solve the central problem. That's all you need to do: defeat that hardest central part of the problem, just enough that you know you're not attempting the impossible. And by doing this, you should also get a clear sense of the scale of the unfinished parts of the problem.

You may need to set a time limit for how long you'll work on the problem. If you're toiling away in your lab for years, you may be overdoing the thing.

How short should this time limit be? Very, very short. A few hours might be enough, a few days should be plenty, and a few weeks is far too long. This isn't "the product to end all products"—this is "your first product." It's not the only time you'll get to try and solve a problem in your life.

It's not a Ph.D. It's a simple product, that one person can build, sell and support. It can be extremely quick.

How long did it take Patrick McKenzie to create his "proof of concept" for the product that would become *Bingo Card Creator*?

> *I cobbled together a solution and released after about four hours.*
> —*Patrick McKenzie*[2]

I wrote the first prototype of *NimbleText* in 20 minutes before breakfast on a very busy Friday morning. And this is not a "humble brag." I'm a notoriously slow programmer. The first version was just *that* simple.

The first version of *Minecraft* was written in six days[3].

Consider Existing Solutions

Based on the earlier steps, the problem we're looking at should be one that your target market is quite familiar with. There may be existing products on the market that address this problem, but there may also be existing approaches that people use for dealing with and overcoming this problem.

Both of these—existing products, and "home-grown" solutions—are worth understanding if you're having trouble solving the problem in a vacuum.

An example that springs to mind is something that occurred in a large software development project I once worked on. Each developer needed to write code on one machine and test it in a separate virtual server. Hence, we needed a way to deploy our compiled binaries from our workstation into the virtual server. There was no team-wide solution handed down to us for tackling this problem. It was something that each person solved individually. As a result, we found that five different developers had developed five different techniques. Two people used two different commercial file-sync tools, one person used an ad-hoc Python script, one used a PowerShell script, one used a batch file. This variety of homegrown solutions will always arise where a real problem exists that hasn't yet been solved in a definitive way. You might ask people in the market, "How do you solve X?" and get 10 different answers from 10 different people.

Consider Academic Research

There is often an academic topic or two that can be applied to your problem which most people are overlooking. More people should read academic papers. Academic papers are fantastic!

You can start by searching *Google Scholar*[4] and see where you end up.

There are three problems with academic papers.

1. Surface level: Understanding the jargon.
2. Deep level: Understanding the underlying theories.
3. Getting access to the complete papers.

Until you understand the jargon, you'll struggle to know the right search terms to narrow down the most relevant papers. It's a bit of a chicken and egg problem. I recommend taking notes and seeking definitions for any special terms you encounter. There may be explanatory blog posts that help you get past this issue. As your comprehension grows you'll be better at finding the right niches within the "fractal-thought-space" of the field you're exploring.

While learning the lingo will help at first, you'll soon get to a point where your ignorance of the foundational theory of a field limits your ability to search it correctly. For this, you need to go back to the classics and the most respected works in the field you're studying. Once you have a passing understanding of the underlying theories, you'll be better equipped to traverse the intellectual mindscape of the academic thinkosphere. Even then you will be stymied by a very simple problem: often the actual papers are just not readily available.

Often it is only the abstract and some bibliographic details that are available for free online. Apart from these tantalizing hints, an impenetrable paywall conceals the full text. The abstract should provide enough information that you can discern the goals and the results of a paper (What did they try? And did they succeed?). Notes on references and related papers should also be available, which are worth following. After surveying several papers at this level, you should know which papers you need to read in depth. One of the things you can readily find is the DOI number, for example: `10.1109/IAT.2005.52`

Here are five ways to gain access to the full text:

1. Pay for it individually. You can expect to pay at least $30 per article.
2. If you have access to a higher-education library, you might be able to read the article for free.
3. You might have a friend with such access. You could potentially get your friend in trouble, so be careful.
4. Contact the author directly. Any time I've done this in the past they have been happy—some are even thrilled!—to provide a PDF copy of their paper. Please be conscious of their time and ask direct questions they can answer quickly.
5. *Sci-Hub* is an online service that bypasses paywalls. This will often breach copyright laws, so you need to

decide for yourself if it's something you're willing to do. Enter the DOI number (example: `10.1109/IAT.2005.52`) into a mirror of *Sci-Hub*[5] and you will receive a complete copy of the article immediately.

Once you've read the right papers, solving the problem for your market may be more about implementing an existing algorithm, rather than inventing a novel approach of your own. After that, you'll provide value by acting as a bridge between the academic terminology and the terminology used by your target market. The challenge (also known as "the curse of knowledge") is to make sure your own terminology continues to make sense to the original market you are addressing and doesn't become as impenetrable as the academic mumbo-jumbo you've hoisted it from.

Attempting the Impossible

What if the problem turns out to be impossible? What do you do then?

When that happens, you do something wonderful, something magical: you give up! You give up on this stupid problem, go back to your target market and look for a new problem. The problem may be solved later, it may even be solved by you, once it's had time to roll around in the back of your mind for a few months or years. But if it's unyielding for now, there are plenty of other problems that your target market is grappling with. Head back and find a new problem.

Once again:

> *If you want to meet your Prince Charming you'll have to kiss a lot of TOADs.*

That's the whole point of this system. Don't get stuck, don't hit your head against a brick wall. Keep moving!

Have You Solved Your Problem?

You've toiled away in your lonely laboratory, and finally emerged, blinking, into the light, cradling your tiny precious prototype.

But what will the people make of it? How will the market respond? Will it go on to be a modest success or a great success? Will it be ignored or will it be despised?

None of these questions can be answered until you "bring it to the market." Exactly what this means and how it can be accomplished is covered in its entirety in the following section.

Again, I'll ask you to follow a process that requires the minimum effort for the maximum information gained. I'll ask you not to rush into mass-marketing and mass-manufacturing of your tender prototype. Instead, I'll ask you to be brave and present it to your market in hope of measuring just one thing: "Demand." The mightiest thing an entrepreneur can ever detect.

CHAPTER 7: TOAD STEP 4: TEST FOR DEMAND

Target • Obstacle • Answer • **Demand**

You Are Here

Once you have a basic solution to your market's problem, it's time to see if you can detect a "demand signal" for your solution.

Here is an overview of the process for finding a demand signal. As before I'll provide you with three techniques.

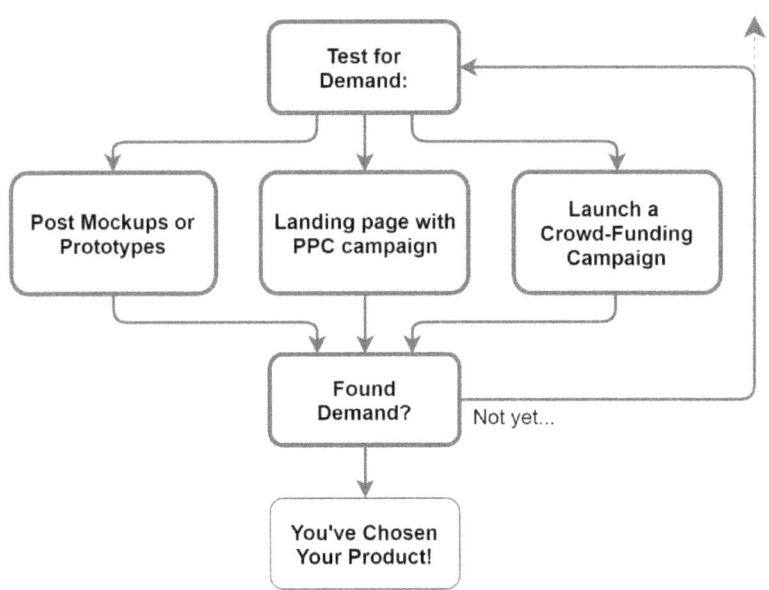

What is a Demand Signal?

If you start telling someone about your solution, and they interrupt, waving money in your face and shouting "Shut Up And Take My Money"[1] then you have definitely found a demand signal.

Most of the time, the signal will be a little more subtle.

Alternative forms of this expression include "Hurry up and ship!", "I need this yesterday!" and some subtle variants include "My friend Jenny was just saying she needed this last week," and "Interesting, but can I just request one minor change..."

Recently I designed a very bad t-shirt and advertised it on twitter. I immediately saw a strong demand signal from my target market, and, because I am a nerd, I cataloged all the different ways that people expressed the demand signal.

I saw many examples of each of the following types of response:

- People explicitly talking about buying it (very clear demand signal.)
- People requesting just one tweak/change/small variation.
- People talking about their reaction in dramatic terms: ("I spat my coffee, and pulled out my credit card immediately," "I'm dying to get my hands on this")
- People recommending it *to* others.

All these responses have one thing in common: people talking! If people are talking, you're doing pretty well. If people consider your idea to be something worth remarking upon then you've found something "remarkable." That's a good start. By far the most common response to all your hard work will be *silence*. Silence is the opposite of a demand signal and it speaks volumes.

Just One Tweak!

I want to spend a moment discussing the meaning of suggested "tweaks." I've observed many times that any remarkable idea will be met with a lot of "helpful suggestions" about how it ought to be done slightly differently. This is so prevalent that you can expect any demand signal will be accompanied by a lot of requests to alter the core product.

If everyone is suggesting a *complete* change of direction, then it may not be a great sign. If many people request the same variation, then it might be worth doing exactly what the market says. With the t-shirt example above, several people wanted the t-shirt to be available in black. I considered this to be slightly outside the core idea of the t-shirt, but I acquiesced and sold a heap of black t-shirts as a result.

Generally, many different requests for a wide variety of small changes are part of a healthy demand signal and strangely symbolic of the way humans express their fondness for a new product idea.

Three Excellent Ways to Test for Demand

There are many ways to test for demand. I suggest you pick whichever one will be the most likely to put your idea in front of your target market. Here are three approaches:

1. Post information to a highly relevant forum
2. Pay for traffic to a landing page describing your product
3. Conduct a crowdfunding campaign

These techniques increase in complexity as we go. It's my belief that the simplest methods work best.

Technique 1: Post Information to a Highly Relevant Forum

From your initial market research, you must know several places online where your target market congregates and engages in market-related discussion.

At one of these places, you can post a description of the problem you are addressing and some artifacts that show your approach. You might post screenshots. You might post a simple mockup, for example using *Balsamiq Mockups*[2].

If a mockup will not convey the nature of your solution, perhaps you need to record a short screencast, or an animated GIF of your invention in action. But keep it simple. Don't over-invest.

Be careful to review the posting guidelines of the forum you are addressing (to what extent do they allow self-promotion?) and use the appropriate tone of voice to suit your audience.

If all you post is a basic outline of your solution then you have posted enough. Extra detail is extraneous. There's no point overselling it. Extra polish is also unnecessary. As Andy Brice says:

> *If you aren't embarrassed by v1.0 you didn't release it early enough*
> —*Andy Brice*[3]

Andy's philosophy applies particularly strongly to these early "demand tests." It only needs to be sufficient to convey the barest outline of the idea.

If your idea is roundly savaged by the forum, consider whether or not that particular forum is a generally negative place. Many forums skew negative. If you told the average forum "I just found a million dollars!" their response would be "Now you'll have to pay more tax," or "It's probably counterfeit." And don't take it to heart. It is the idea that was savaged, not you personally.

But if you've done your research and you're addressing a problem the audience are passionate about, there is a reasonable chance you will get a strong positive reaction. In which case you can immediately commit to your idea and leap into the next phase.

Technique 2: Landing Page with Pay-Per-Click Campaign

Another approach for measuring demand is to pay for traffic to a landing page and measure the behavior of your visitors.

You might buy *AdWords*[4] through Google. Or you might advertise on *Facebook*[5] or at *StackOverflow*[6] or another advertising network, or buy a niche advertisement spot at your website of choice. It's crucial that your advertisement is highly targeted to your chosen audience, who are likely to experience the exact problem you are attempting to solve.

The advantage of this approach is that you will have numbers to analyze. The disadvantage is that these numbers alone are unlikely to give you a clear demand signal. You might be able to tell, for example, that $100 of advertising expenditure brings you 20 visitors who sign up to hear more about your product. But it's hard to get richer information, the sort of "market chatter" that reveals more about the passion that your product does (or does not) inspire and helps guide you toward a more successful product. If you have people sign up, then you can talk to them, one at a time, and ask for feedback on your product idea. By this stage they are so highly qualified as potential customers that they are likely to give very useful feedback.

You can establish a simple landing page website by using a paid service such as *LeadPages*[7] or *Unbounce*[8]. *LeadPages* will set you back about $300, and that's before you've paid for traffic. Their cheapest tier is listed as $25 per month, but look closer and you'll see this is paid *annually* so you're looking at spending at least $300. *Unbounce* is $79 per month, so you can try out an idea more cheaply there, but I see that as a heavy outlay for an as-yet unproven idea. (You might get away with just using the free 30 day trial at *Unbounce*, but it's a challenging approach to take.) With any of the paid services, they hold onto any customer list that you acquire, and you can end up quite limited with how you're able to access the customer list you've worked so hard to acquire.

If you can build websites, then you can build your own landing page without any help from *LeadPages* and friends. I've put a lot of work into researching the cheapest way to make your own landing pages, without paying for **anything**: no payment for hosting, data-collection, or templates. Eventually, I've happened upon a technique that lets you do it all, on your own custom domain (over HTTPS even, if you know how important that has become) without paying any money, other than the unavoidable cost of registering your own domain (about $10 per year). The overview of the technique is that you use *GitHub Pages*[9] to host a static webpage, based on a stylish free template, that stores data in a *Google Sheet*[10]. The technical details of making this technique sing are too specific to include inside a printed book, so I've put them online at:

YourFirstProduct.com/Info/free-email-capture [11]

There are various repositories of attractive, free templates online, but it will take an investment of several hours to find one that is modern, stylish and suitable for your audience. My general rule when selecting a template (or a font) is that however much time you predict it will take: double it. Once you've found an attractive template, you also need to customize the verbiage, the wording, the "copy" (as the professionals call it) to suit your message. Much has been written on the topic of copy. The number one rule is targeting your copy toward your audience, and it is for this reason that the TOAD starts by determining the target customer. Once you have a laser focus on the end customer (and research to boot) you can make sure your language is pitched at them personally.

Remember that you are not yet committed to your idea. You should not over-commit when building this demand test. If your demand test succeeds you will have plenty of opportunities to build an amazing website later. Don't waste time now over-testing an idea that may fail the demand test. Remember also, that when you are testing your next idea you can reuse anything you built for this test. But if you give money to *LeadPages* (for example) you can't reuse that money later.

Technique 3: Conduct a Crowdfunding Campaign

Another approach you can use to test for demand is the exciting new world of crowd-funding. The two most popular crowdfunding sites are *Kickstarter*[12] and *GoFundMe*[13]. *GoFundMe* is focused on donations for personal causes and is not appropriate for testing product ideas. Hence, in this section I'll talk exclusively about *Kickstarter*.

Kickstarter uses an "All or Nothing" funding goal; if pledges don't meet your funding goal on time you get no money at all, and your potential customer gets their money back. This is part of the magic of *Kickstarter*: the sense of urgency drives backers and project creators to work their butts off. It also means that your potential customers have a vested interest in helping to promote your product.

Why a Kickstarter Campaign is a Good Idea

There are a number of reasons why a *Kickstarter* campaign is so appealing:

1. People are not just asked if they like your idea: they are asked to put money into it. Data about purchasing-potential provides a very clear signal when it is already tied to real money.
2. *Kickstarter* make the process pretty straightforward (that's their job)
3. You are asked to put forward a concrete financial goal, with a strict calendar deadline. That's a great forcing function for keeping you tied to an attainable outcome.
4. If you fall short of the goal, you receive none of the money. This is a good way to ensure you don't press on, wasting your life on a dead-end idea. It frees you up to try a new approach.
5. It forces you to share your idea, to let go of your idea, to put it out there in the world, to take a chance.
6. People are partly motivated out of conspicuous social factors (you can see what projects people have backed). Hence, if your product involves a social benefit or an altruistic purpose, people will be more likely to want to share that with their friends, which draws in more traffic.

Why a Kickstarter Campaign is a Bad Idea

A *Kickstarter* campaign has these drawbacks:

1. A *Kickstarter* campaign is much more complex than the two previous methods for demand-testing
2. Money received from a *Kickstarter* campaign is investment money, not product sales. A humble first product shouldn't need investment upfront. You need sales. So, it can be a distraction from your final goal.
3. Many *Kickstarter* projects involve physical goods, so the audience is not ready-made for a pure digital product. For many software products, for example, it can be hard to provide the immediate visual appeal that you see in most successful *Kickstarter* campaigns.
4. *Kickstarter* campaigns are generally based on creative arts. To illustrate, here's the first 7 of their 15 categories: Art, Comics, Crafts, Dance, Design, Fashion, Film & Video. A pure software product would be shelved in the Technology category (or the Web category), which has a Software and a Web subcategory (alongside 14 other subcategories).
5. If, after you have launched your *Kickstarter* campaign, you find from early feedback that you need to alter your product offering (even in a small way), it can be hard to do if you've already raised money. If some people ask for a refund at that point, you've lost the fees and credit card charges from their pledge.
6. You need to pay *Kickstarter*'s fees[14], taxes and credit card fees, these can eat up 10 to 20 percent of your gross income.

And here's a point which is neither a plus or minus, but an "interesting" (in the language of Edward De Bono[15])

Only one-third of *Kickstarter* campaigns meet their funding goals. Of those that do, if they make it to 60% of their funding goal they have a 98% chance of going the whole way. There is compelling evidence[16] that if you've made strong efforts to bring backers in initially, but have not reached 25% of your funding goal after two weeks, you have only a slim chance of the campaign succeeding. This gives you an opportunity to "Fail Fast" and start working on a new or modified idea sooner. There are plenty more TOADs in the swamp.

Have You Met Your Goal?

At this stage, if things went well, you will have a list of real people who would be willing to pay money for the product you intend to build. I'll talk about your next steps in the final chapters.

But it's possible, and even likely, that things did *not* go well. Your solution did not cause any strong response from the target market and you need to head "back to the drawing board" to revise your offering. You may improve your prototype, improve the way you've described it, or you might make more drastic changes. You might look for a different problem to solve, or even switch to a different target market.

Experience gained from moving through this process even once will accelerate your speed on subsequent attempts. Product development is a skill and it takes practice to achieve proficiency at any skill.

CHAPTER 8: NEXT STEPS

Now you've found an idea and you have 10 or more customers lined up, begging to pay good money for the thing. After that it's plain sailing.

All you need to do is choose a product name, something catchy, relevant, and charming. Make sure the ".com" domain is available, snap it up immediately as you slap together a neat looking website for collecting contact details of prospective customers. Decide on a business model, develop the actual product, choose which features to defer, which features are free, and which are premium. Perform alpha and beta testing, set up payment processing, decide on a price, make sure all your legal requirements are taken care of and launch the product (this one is a must!) Run targeted advertisements, optimize the analytics and SEO of your site, build lead magnets, free gifts, and educational content that draw the customers in from every corner of the globe. Evolve your product based on meaningful conversations and solid metrics (without destroying its initial appeal!) Support the product in a cost-effective manner even as hordes of hard to please customers storm over the barricades. Evolve the pricing structure into a well-thought-out set of tiers that capture surplus capital, while keeping an eye out for new product opportunities. Oh, and try to relax and catch up with old friends whenever you can.

Look out for more books at YourFirstProduct.com. There is much to say about the journey ahead.

APPENDIX A: TOAD OVERVIEW

A print-friendly copy of all flowcharts is available from:
YourFirstProduct.com/Tools/TOAD

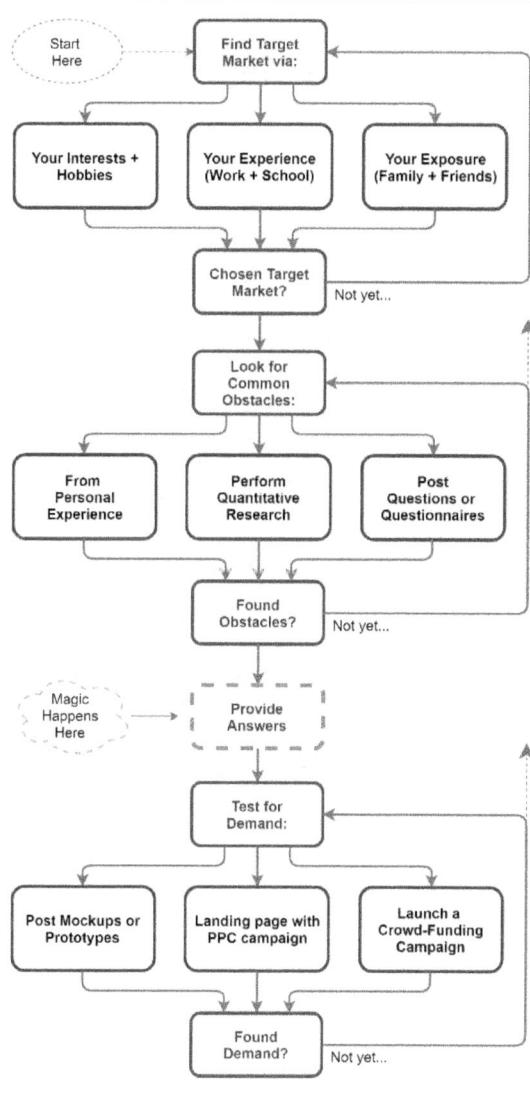

APPENDIX B: REFERENCES

Chapter 2

1. Rob Walling, "9 Entrepreneurs Reveal How They Validated Their Business Idea," see https://www.entrepreneur.com/article/233408
2. Ray Bradbury, "Jump Off the Cliff and Build Your Wings on the Way Down," see https://quoteinvestigator.com/2012/06/17/cliff-wings
3. Jason Cohen, "Yes, but who said they'd actually BUY the damn thing?" see https://blog.asmartbear.com/customer-validation.html

Chapter 4

1. Paul Graham, "How to Get Startup Ideas," see http://paulgraham.com/startupideas.html
2. Marc Andreessen, "The Only Thing That Matters," see https://pmarchive.com/guide_to_startups_part4.html
3. Slava Akhmechet, "How to pick startup ideas," see http://www.defmacro.org/2015/02/25/startup-ideas.html
4. Lloyd, see cinematic masterpiece "Dumb & Dumber," 1994.
5. Reddit, see https://reddit.com
6. Subreddit search, see https://reddit.com/subreddits/search

7. CSharp subreddit, see https://reddit.com/r/csharp
8. Dotnet subreddit, see https://reddit.com/r/dotnet
9. Proggit, see https://www.reddit.com/r/programming
10. Redsim, see https://anvaka.github.io/redsim
11. Reddit Metrics, see http://redditmetrics.com/r/dotnet
12. Later For Reddit, see https://dashboard.laterforreddit.com

Chapter 5

1. Paul Graham, "How to Get Startup Ideas," see http://paulgraham.com/startupideas.html
2. David S. Platt, see book "Why Software Sucks...and What You Can Do About It."
3. TimeSnapper, see http://TimeSnapper.com
4. NimbleText, see http://NimbleText.com
5. NextAction, see http://www.TimeSnapper.com/NextAction
6. Amy Hoy, "Sales Safari," see https://stackingthebricks.com/vintage-sales-safari-in-action
7. Amy Hoy and Alex Hillman's "30x500 Academy" see https://30x500.com/academy
8. Wikipedia, "Computer-assisted qualitative data analysis software," see https://en.wikipedia.org/wiki/Computer-assisted_qualitative_data_analysis_software
9. EverNote, see https://evernote.com
10. Microsoft OneNote, see https://www.onenote.com
11. Notepad++, see https://notepad-plus-plus.org
12. Flappy Bird, see

CHOOSE YOUR FIRST PRODUCT

      https://en.wikipedia.org/wiki/Flappy_Bird
13. Not Henry Ford, "Quote Investigator: My Customers Would Have Asked For a Faster Horse," see https://quoteinvestigator.com/2011/07/28/ford-faster-horse
14. Hacker News, see https://New.Ycombinator.com
15. Google Forms, see https://www.google.com/forms/about
16. Google Sheets, see https://www.google.com/sheets/about
17. Survey Monkey, see https://www.surveymonkey.com
18. TypeForm, see https://www.typeform.com

Chapter 6.

1. Murray Gell-Mann, "The Feynman Algorithm," see http://wiki.c2.com/?FeynmanAlgorithm
2. Patrick McKenzie, "Start Here if You're New," see https://www.kalzumeus.com/start-here-if-youre-new
3. Minecraft Version History, see https://minecraft.gamepedia.com/Version_history#Pre-classic
4. Google Scholar, see https://scholar.google.com
5. SciHub Mirror, see http://Sci-Hub.hk

Chapter 7

1. Futurama, Season 6 Episode 3, "Attack of the Killer App"
2. Balsamiq Mockups, see

https://balsamiq.com/products
3. Andy Brice, "If you aren't embarrassed by v1.0 you didn't release it early enough," see https://successfulsoftware.net/2007/08/07/if-you-arent-embarrassed-by-v10-you-didnt-release-it-early-enough
4. Google Adwords, see https://Adwords.Google.com
5. Facebook Advertising, see https://Facebook.com/Ads
6. Stack Overflow Advertising, see https://www.stackoverflowbusiness.com/engagement
7. LeadPages, see https://www.leadpages.net
8. Unbounce, see https://unbounce.com
9. GitHub Pages, see https://pages.github.com
10. Google Sheets, see https://www.google.com/sheets/about
11. Leon Bambrick, "Completely FREE Email Capture Without Limitations," see https://yourfirstproduct.com/Info/free-email-capture
12. KickStarter, https://www.kickstarter.com
13. GoFundMe, https://www.gofundme.com
14. KickStarter Fees, see https://www.kickstarter.com/help/fees
15. Edward De Bono, "Plus Minus Interesting" see book "De Bono's Thinking Course"
16. Stonemaier Games, "Kickstarter Lesson #49: To Cancel or to Finish" see https://stonemaiergames.com/kickstarter-lesson-49-to-cancel-or-to-finish

APPENDIX C: IMAGE CREDITS

TOAD logo based on "The Frog Prince" by Gamze Genc Celik from *the Noun Project*, ID 1194602.

Chapter 2

- The Sword in the Stone, Creative-Commons-Zero, see https://pixabay.com/en/excalibur-legend-sword-england-145647

Chapter 4

- Medieval Market Place, detail from "Grosse Kirchweih," an engraving by Sebald Beham, 1535.
- Modified still from "*Dumb & Dumber*," 1994.

Chapter 5

- Diamond image, see https://openclipart.org/detail/125695/diamant-diamond
- Flappy bird screenshot from *Flappy Bird* by Dong Nguyen of dotGEARS
- Meme image from *Futurama*, Season 6 Episode 3, "Attack of the Killer App"

All other illustrations by the author.

ABOUT THE AUTHOR

Leon is the author of secretGeek.net, the creator of NimbleText and NimbleSET, and the co-creator of TimeSnapper.com.

Follow him on twitter @secretGeek
or email Leon@YourFirstProduct.com

He lives in Brisbane, Australia,
with an awesome family.

www.ingramcontent.com/pod-product-compliance
Lightning Source LLC
Chambersburg PA
CBHW050309230526
45471CB00005B/2096